x973.2   Fritz, Jean
          Who's that stepping on Plymouth
F91w   Rock? Illus. by J. B. Handelsman.
          Coward 1975
            30p illus

3 1192 00240 5536

1.Pilgrim Fathers 2.U.S.—History—Colo-
nial period I.Title

INTERIM   P9-BZS-794

DATE DUE

NOV. 29. 1973   NOV   6 1982

      DEC   5 1979   JUL 1 3 1983

      SEP 1 3 1980
      DEC 1 0 1980 DEC 1 8 1983

      MAR   3 1981   OCT 8   1984
J
      JUN 2 1 1982

Evanston Public Library
Evanston, Illinois

Each reader is responsible for all
books or other materials taken on his
card, and for any fines or fees
charged for overdues, damages, or
loss.

DEMCO

Who's that Stepping on Plymouth Rock?

Who's that Stepping on Plymouth Rock?

by JEAN FRITZ

illustrated by J. B. HANDELSMAN

x 973.2
F91w

Coward, McCann & Geoghegan, Inc.
New York

EVANSTON PUBLIC LIBRARY
CHILDREN'S DEPARTMENT
1703 ORRINGTON AVENUE
EVANSTON, ILLINOIS 60201

Bt476

Text copyright © 1975 by Jean Fritz
Illustrations copyright © 1975 by J. B. Handelsman
All rights reserved.
This book, or parts thereof, may not be reproduced in
any form without permission in writing from the
publishers. Published simultaneously in Canada by
Longman Canada Limited, Toronto.
SBN: GB-698-30578-7
SBN: TR-698-20325-9
Library of Congress Catalog Card Number: 74-30593
PRINTED IN THE UNITED STATES OF AMERICA
07211

TO CHARLOTTE LANE

On the bay that would later become the harbor front of Plymouth, Massachusetts, there was one large rock and only one rock. When the tide came in, the rock was slapped by waves; when the tide went out, the rock sat high and lonely on the beach. Sometimes sea gulls landed on the rock, folded their wings, and stared at the empty sea. Sometimes Indians came to the rock. Perhaps they cleaned their fish on it. Perhaps not. The rock didn't say.

Then along came 1620. And on the twenty-second day of December along came the *Mayflower* with 104 Pilgrims looking for a place to land. (They weren't called Pilgrims then; for a long time they were known simply as the First Comers.)

Anyway, there they were coming ashore and there on the shore was the rock, but if they got together, no one made a record of it. The First Comers didn't scratch their initials on the rock; they didn't put up a marker that said, "We stepped here." Not one of the 104 ever wrote down a word about the rock. (Of course, they may have been too busy trying to keep alive.)

For the next 121 years the rock sat silent on the harbor front, not doing a thing to make history. Then suddenly in 1741 the rock became a subject for conversation. A wharf was going to be built at

the very spot where the rock was. Indeed the builders, since they couldn't move the rock, planned to build a wharf over and around it, leaving a hole in the planks for the top of the rock to poke through.

"But you can't do that," some people said. "It's the only big rock we have. It's a landmark."

They ran to Eel River, where Elder Thomas
Faunce lived, and they carried him down the beach
in his chair. Elder Faunce was 95 years old, and his
father had known some of the First Comers. They
pointed to the rock. "It is a landmark, isn't it?"
they asked. "Didn't your pa tell you it was a landmark?"

Elder Faunce nodded slowly. "Had to do with
the First Comers," he said. Suddenly his face
clouded over. "They don't aim to bury that rock,
do they? Why, that's where the First Comers first
landed." He pointed a shaky finger. "On that
rock. That selfsame rock. They steered their boat to
it and out they stepped."

Everyone agreed that Elder Faunce was remark-
ably clearheaded for his age. Still, not everyone
agreed about the rock.

The Aldens agreed. They said Yes, John Alden
had been the first of the First Comers to step on the
rock. The Winslows said that Mary Winslow had
been the first. But since neither John nor Mary had
been in the first boatload to go ashore, it is hard to
see how they could have been right.

In general, seafaring men disagreed. They said the rock story was a barrel of nonsense. The First Comers would have been out of their heads, they said, to have steered for a rock when there was the sheltered mouth of a brook nearby.

In any case, the people of Plymouth should have saved their breath to cool their porridge. The wharf builders paid no attention to their talk. The wharf was built just as planned, with the top part of the rock coming up for air through the planks. Soon the sight seemed natural to the people of Plymouth. No one talked about the rock anymore, but they all walked around it. Everyone. Travelers, sailors,

children, cats, dogs, merchants, loafers, townspeople waving to outgoing ships, townspeople
greeting incoming ones. Horses sidestepped it,
boys and girls climbed over it, barrels bumped
against it. For 33 years people brushed by it,
stamped around it, and knocked into it without
a thought for the First Comers or their First Steps.
The rock, as usual, had nothing to say.

Then in 1769 some of the descendants of the
First Comers decided to celebrate the anniversary of
the Landing. From now on, they said, December 22
would be called Forefathers Day. There would be a
church service, a town parade, and a meal of
thanksgiving. They might even shoot off a cannon
if they could think of something special to shoot it
off about. In Boston people had an elm tree still

growing on their common that had been there when the first Colonists arrived. They were always celebrating that old elm. But what did Plymouth have?

Deacon Ephraim Spooner spoke up. Plymouth had a rock, he said. Although he'd only been six years old at the time, Deacon Spooner had been present when Elder Faunce had told the rock story.

Now others recalled the story too. The Aldens, of course, told it one way and the Winslows told it another way, and seafaring men thought it was all a barrel of nonsense. Still, no one could say for certain that the story wasn't true, and everyone agreed that some of the First Comers must have stood, sat, or leaned on the rock at one time or another. After all, it *was* the only big rock on the shore. It *had* been there to welcome the First Comers. Wasn't that enough to make it famous? Of course. They would call it Forefathers Rock and plant it squarely in American history where it belonged.

13

So the celebration took place—marching, singing, prayers, cannon fire, and a feast of nine courses that included whortleberry pudding, succotash, clams, oysters, eels, codfish, venison, apple pie, and cranberry tarts. Then, full of food and patriotism, the people of Plymouth walked down to the beach to pay their respects to the old rock.

But the celebration didn't change Plymouth or
the rock. The next day people went down to the
wharf and there was the rock right in their path, the
same as usual. They found it hard to keep history in
mind. So they scratched mud from their boots onto
the rock just as they always had. They rested on the
rock if they felt like it. They used the rock as a
setting-down place for whatever they were deliver-
ing to the wharf or carrying away from it. A bag of
rice, a keg of molasses, a crate of chickens. Of

course, it was a shameful business. The only famous rock on the North American continent, and
there it was being treated like common granite. A
monument to liberty, and there it was imprisoned
in a wharf, hemmed in at the neck like a man with
his head in the stocks.

Year after year on Forefathers Day the people of Plymouth honored their rock, but on other days they gave it little thought. What could they do? The rock weighed many tons and had been where it was for 35,000 years because no one had figured out how to move it. A glacier had dropped it there in the first place, and as far as anyone could see, it would take another glacier to move it. Meanwhile there were more important matters to attend to. The whole country was getting deeper and deeper into an argument about the rights of the Colonies and the rights of England. By 1774 tempers were boiling. Half the people were angry at the other half, and there was talk of war with England. In Plymouth people were so divided they could not even agree on how to celebrate Forefathers Day. The Tories (those on England's side) said the celebration should be private. Some said there should be no celebration. But the liberty men (those on the side of the Colonies) said there should be the biggest and best celebration Plymouth had ever had. If ever the town needed to be reminded of the First Comers, they said,

it was now. If ever the country needed to be reminded of Plymouth, the birthplace of liberty, it was this year. And the biggest thing they could think of to do was to move the rock.

As a first step, they removed those planks of the wharf that interfered with the rock. Then on the morning of December 22 the biggest, strongest liberty men who could be found assembled at the waterfront with large jackscrews, iron chains, and thirty yoke of oxen. The people of Plymouth were

there too. Some were betting that the rock couldn't be moved. A few said it shouldn't be moved. But most thought it would be a great stroke for liberty if the rock were moved. So as the rock was slowly elevated from its bed by jackscrews, the observers tensed their muscles and set their jaws. The thirty yoke of oxen leaned into their work, straining forward, shoulders bulging. "Here she comes," the people grunted. "Here she comes."

But the rock didn't come. Just as it was raised to the proper height so it could be hoisted onto the cart that stood ready, the rock fell and broke in two. Crosswise. Like two halves of a layer cake.

"Ahhhhhhhhhh!" The whole town let out one great community sigh.

The oxen shifted their legs and looked back over their shoulders. The liberty men studied the rock. The top part of the rock alone was an impressive size. And after all, if any first stepping had been done, they said, it had been done on the top. So leaving the bottom of the rock on the sand where it

had always been, the liberty men and the oxen went to work on the top.

"Here she comes," the people grunted. "Here she comes."

This time the rock did come. Safely onto the cart. The people let out three loud huzzahs and followed the cart, the rock, the oxen, and the liberty men to Meeting House Square. Carefully, with more maneuvering and more grunting, the rock was lowered to the foot of an elm tree near the town's liberty pole. The Standish Guards fired a salute, the people cheered, and at the top of the liberty pole the liberty flag waved the famous words of Patrick Henry: LIBERTY OR DEATH.

Now there were two Forefathers Rocks, but no one paid any attention to the bottom part. The wharf builders built their wharf back over it, leaving a place for the top to poke up. Most of the top, of course, was up at the square, so only a bump showed. Wagon wheels straddled it, people walked over it, crates were dragged across it. It was so muddied up that if a stranger asked to see it, someone would have to sweep it off.

But at the square the top part reclined in fame against the elm tree.

Time passed. Americans fought their war with England and won it. From now on they had a history of their own. Not a long history, to be sure, but they had to make the best of what they had. So they talked about their history and they wrote about it. It was said that anyone who could hold a pen these days felt called on to write something about America's past. But sometimes talking and writing were not enough. Sometimes people wanted to point to something solid and say, "There. That's a place where it all began." The rock at Plymouth was about the most solid thing Americans could find. So from all over the country people came to see Plymouth Rock. Sometimes, if no one was looking, they chipped bits off to take home as souvenirs.

After a while the people of Plymouth decided they couldn't leave such a famous rock lying around loose under an elm tree. So in 1834 they moved it to the front of Pilgrim Hall, a new building that had been erected by the Pilgrim Society in the center of town. Of course, the moving wasn't easy. This time the cart that had the rock in it tipped over, and the rock fell out and broke in two.

Up and down. Like two hunks of cake with some crumbs left over scattered about the street.

"Ahhhhhhhhhhhh!"

Naturally the people of Plymouth groaned, but there was nothing to do but pick up the pieces and go on. (Souvenir hunters gathered up the crumbs.)

Eventually the two pieces were cemented together and a fence of iron pickets was put around it. Each picket was inscribed with the name of one of the signers of the Mayflower Compact.

More and more Americans came to see Plymouth Rock. They were proud as they looked down through the iron pickets at the rock with the date 1620 painted across it. But they were also surprised. *That* little chunk of rock was what the Pilgrims had stepped on?

Of course, the visitors had it explained to them. That chunk was only part of the rock. If they wanted to see the other part, they'd have to go down to the wharf. They might have to move aside some bags of salt to see it; they might have to ask a fisherman to drag away a mess of fish, but it was there, all right. A little bump. The rest lay under the wharf.

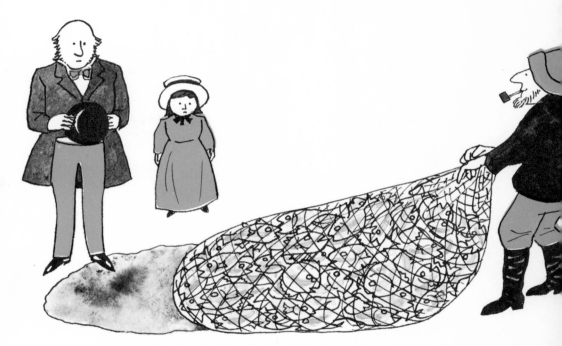

It was too bad. A piece of solid American history cut in two—one part getting all the credit, the other part overlooked. After a while the members of the Pilgrim Society got tired of explaining and apologizing, so they began buying up the wharf, a warehouse at a time, until by 1859 they owned the upper part of the wharf. Then they tore it down. And there was the rock, free again. Big and solid as ever. Standing in the sand where it had been for all those thousands of years.

Of course, there was nothing special to mark it. No iron fence around it. No *1620* painted across it. What it needed was a monument. And that's what it got. In 1867 an imposing stone canopy was raised over it: four tall columns with iron rail gates between the columns and a heavy arched dome over the top. In the daytime the gates were left open so people could step down on the rock right where the Pilgrims had stepped. Many people didn't know that the Pilgrims could never really have stepped there. If the Pilgrims had done any stepping, it was on the top part of the rock, but that was up a hill and out of the way.

It was too bad. A piece of American history cut in two—one part enshrined in a stone monument, the other part stuck behind a little iron fence.

After a while the people of Plymouth decided that the two parts of the rock couldn't go on like that. It had been more than 100 years since they'd started dragging the rock around town, but there was no help for it; it would have to be done again. So in 1880 they moved the upper part of the rock down to the lower part of the rock and they cemented them together. One rock under one canopy. They washed off the *1620* that had been painted on the top rock and they cut a new *1620* on it that would last as long as the rock lasted. What more could anyone do for a rock?

Nothing. Everyone was satisfied. At least for a while. Then along came 1920. This was the 300th anniversary of the Landing, and of course, for such an important event something would have to be done. The biggest thing anyone could think of was to move the rock.

What the rock needed, people said, was a bigger monument and nicer surroundings. So on Forefathers Day, 1920, out came the iron chains again, out came a crane, out came the people of Plymouth to cheer the rock on its new journey. It wasn't going far. Just to an empty lot where it was to wait for the waterfront to be landscaped and for a new monument to be built.

It waited almost a year for its monument—a grand structure that looked like a Greek temple with twelve columns surrounding it. Some people thought that the rock seemed to look smaller in its new home than it had in the old days. But small or not, more and more people who studied the history of Plymouth came to agree with Elder Thomas Faunce and Deacon Spooner. Even some seafaring men agreed. The rock really might have been the place where the First Steps were taken.

But Americans weren't going to argue about it anymore. They had a piece of solid history and they were proud of it. Every year people come to see the rock. Presidents, Vice Presidents, visitors from abroad, famous people and ordinary people. Approx-

imately 1,250,000 people come every summer to see Plymouth Rock. Most of them are mothers and fathers, boys and girls.

And celebrations? Of course, On the 350th anniversary of the Landing 100,000 people watched the grand opening-day parade. Every summer there are parades, and at Thanksgiving there is always a celebration to honor the Pilgrims. Indeed there are so many celebrations that Forefathers Day is no longer the special day it once was. Still, it is not entirely forgotten. A small band of people get up at five o'clock in the morning of Forefathers Day, put on tall

Pilgrim hats, and march down to the rock, dragging a small cannon behind them. About the time the sun is rising over the harbor, they shoot off their cannon and then they go home.

The rock stays where it is. For a few hours it is alone again with the sea gulls and the tides, almost the way it was long ago before the First Comers took their First Steps.

EVANSTON PUBLIC LIBRARY
CHILDREN'S DEPARTMENT
1703 ORRINGTON AVENUE
EVANSTON, ILLINOIS 60201